FOR AN ORGANIZED
TO-DO LIST,
Use This Planner!

ACTIVINOTES

Activinotes

DAILY JOURNALS, PLANNERS, NOTEBOOKS AND OTHER BLANK BOOKS

Weekly Planner

MONDAY	TUESDAY	WEDNESDAY	To Do List

THURSDAY	FRIDAY	SATURDAY	To Buy List

SUNDAY	To Do List

Weekly Planner

Weekly Planner

Weekly Planner

MONDAY	TUESDAY	WEDNESDAY	To Do List

THURSDAY	FRIDAY	SATURDAY	To Buy List

SUNDAY	To Do List

Weekly Planner

Weekly Planner

Weekly Planner

MONDAY	TUESDAY	WEDNESDAY	To Do List

THURSDAY	FRIDAY	SATURDAY	To Buy List

SUNDAY	To Do List

Weekly Planner

Weekly Planner

Weekly Planner

MONDAY	TUESDAY	WEDNESDAY	To Do List

THURSDAY	FRIDAY	SATURDAY	To Buy List

SUNDAY	To Do List

Weekly Planner

Weekly Planner

Weekly Planner

MONDAY	TUESDAY	WEDNESDAY	To Do List

THURSDAY	FRIDAY	SATURDAY	To Buy List

SUNDAY	To Do List

Weekly Planner

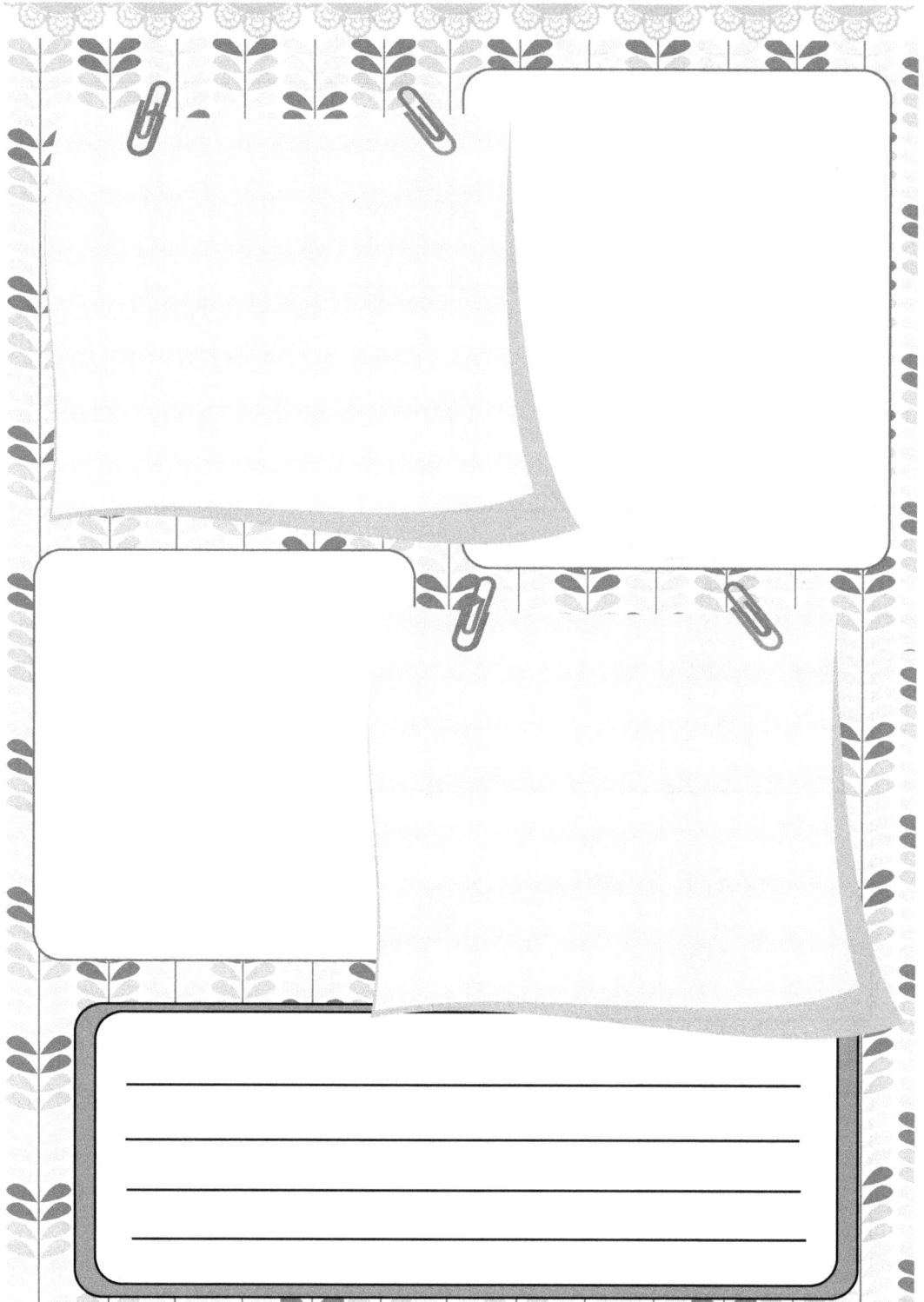

Weekly Planner

Weekly Planner

MONDAY	TUESDAY	WEDNESDAY	To Do List

THURSDAY	FRIDAY	SATURDAY	To Buy List

SUNDAY	To Do List

Weekly Planner

Weekly Planner

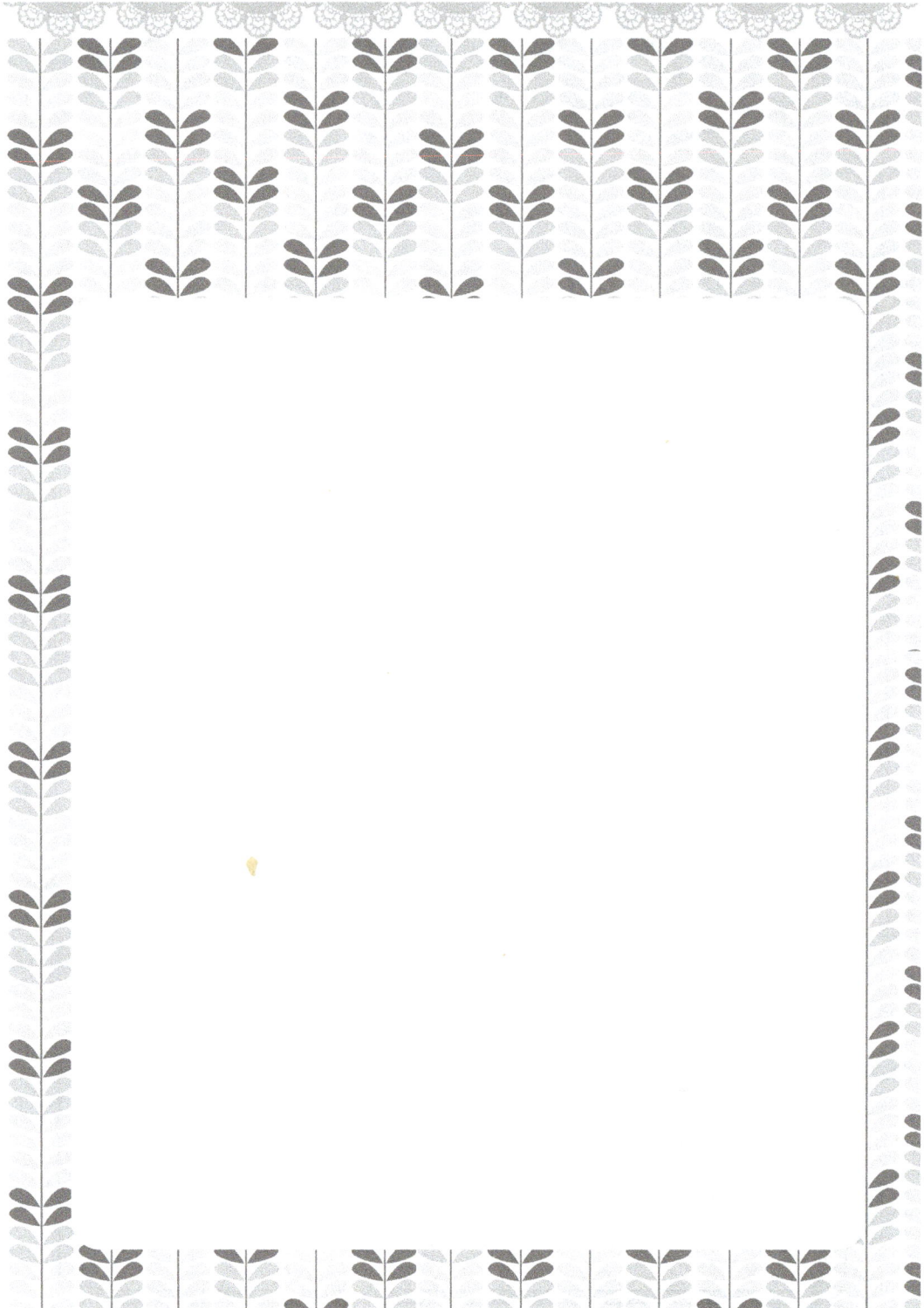

Weekly Planner

MONDAY	TUESDAY	WEDNESDAY	To Do List

THURSDAY	FRIDAY	SATURDAY	To Buy List

SUNDAY	To Do List

Weekly Planner

Weekly Planner

Weekly Planner

MONDAY	TUESDAY	WEDNESDAY	To Do List

THURSDAY	FRIDAY	SATURDAY	To Buy List

SUNDAY	To Do List

Weekly Planner

Weekly Planner

Weekly Planner

MONDAY	TUESDAY	WEDNESDAY	To Do List

THURSDAY	FRIDAY	SATURDAY	To Buy List

SUNDAY	To Do List

Weekly Planner

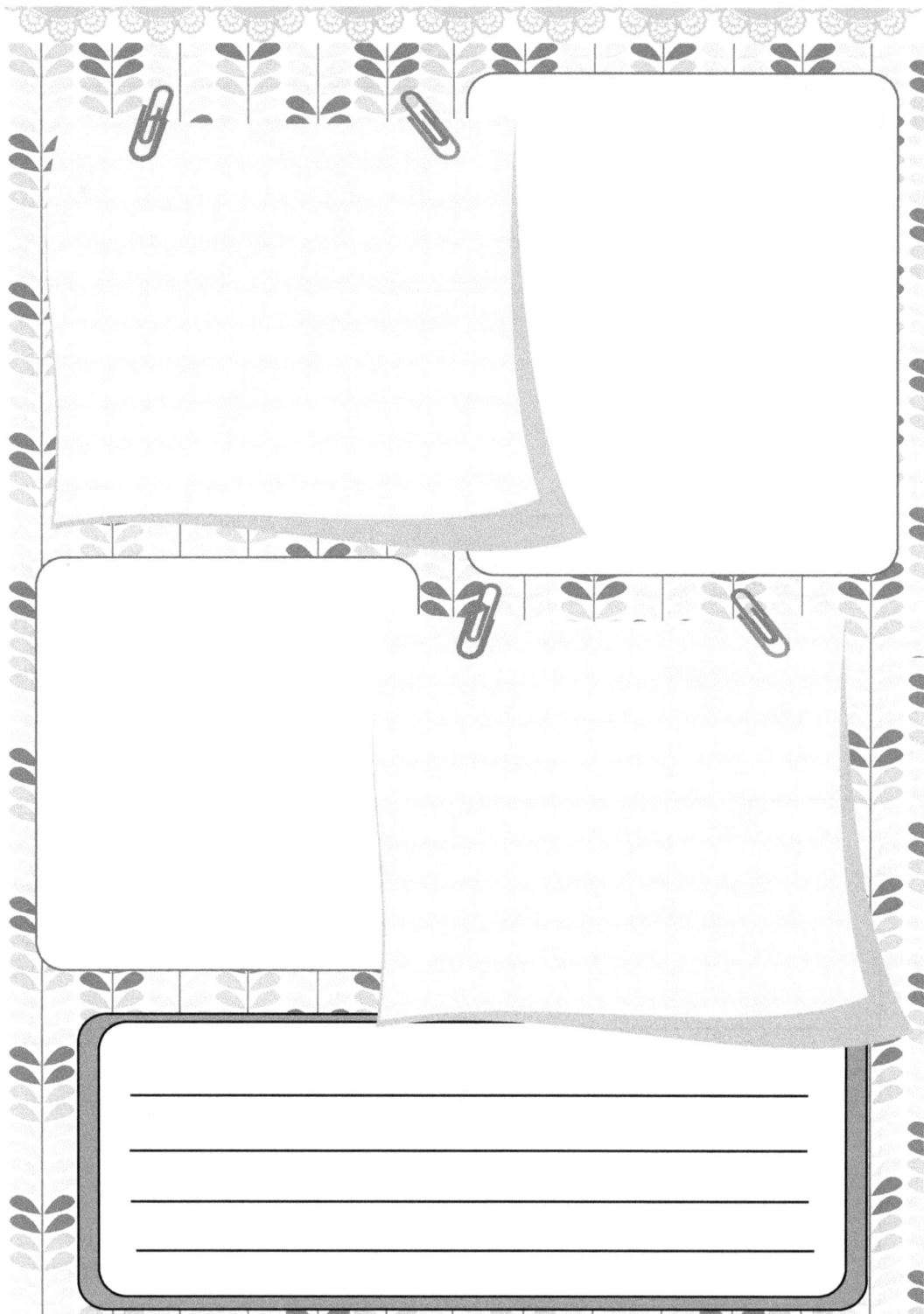

Weekly Planner

Weekly Planner

MONDAY	TUESDAY	WEDNESDAY	To Do List

THURSDAY	FRIDAY	SATURDAY	To Buy List

SUNDAY	To Do List

Weekly Planner

Weekly Planner

Weekly Planner

MONDAY	TUESDAY	WEDNESDAY	To Do List

THURSDAY	FRIDAY	SATURDAY	To Buy List

SUNDAY	To Do List

Weekly Planner

Weekly Planner

Weekly Planner

MONDAY	TUESDAY	WEDNESDAY	To Do List

THURSDAY	FRIDAY	SATURDAY	To Buy List

SUNDAY	To Do List

Weekly Planner

Weekly Planner

Weekly Planner

MONDAY	TUESDAY	WEDNESDAY	To Do List

THURSDAY	FRIDAY	SATURDAY	To Buy List

SUNDAY	To Do List

Weekly Planner

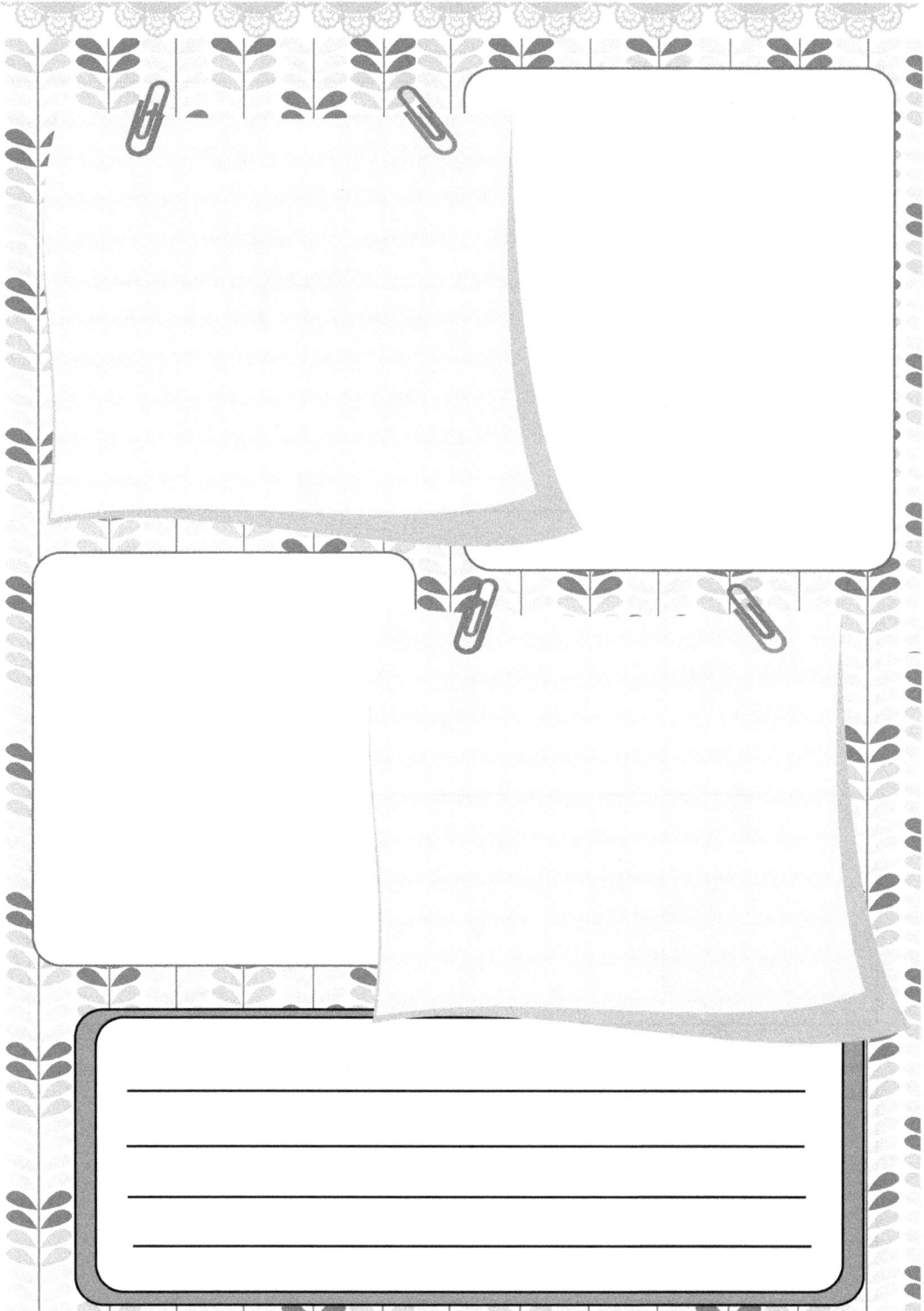

Weekly Planner

Weekly Planner

MONDAY	TUESDAY	WEDNESDAY	To Do List

THURSDAY	FRIDAY	SATURDAY	To Buy List

SUNDAY	To Do List

Weekly Planner

Weekly Planner

Weekly Planner

MONDAY	TUESDAY	WEDNESDAY	To Do List

THURSDAY	FRIDAY	SATURDAY	To Buy List

SUNDAY	To Do List

Weekly Planner

Weekly Planner

Weekly Planner

MONDAY	TUESDAY	WEDNESDAY	To Do List

THURSDAY	FRIDAY	SATURDAY	To Buy List

SUNDAY	To Do List

Weekly Planner

Weekly Planner

Weekly Planner

MONDAY	TUESDAY	WEDNESDAY	To Do List

THURSDAY	FRIDAY	SATURDAY	To Buy List

SUNDAY	To Do List

Weekly Planner

Weekly Planner

Weekly Planner

MONDAY	TUESDAY	WEDNESDAY	To Do List

THURSDAY	FRIDAY	SATURDAY	To Buy List

SUNDAY	To Do List

Weekly Planner

Weekly Planner

Weekly Planner

MONDAY	TUESDAY	WEDNESDAY	To Do List

THURSDAY	FRIDAY	SATURDAY	To Buy List

SUNDAY	To Do List

Weekly Planner

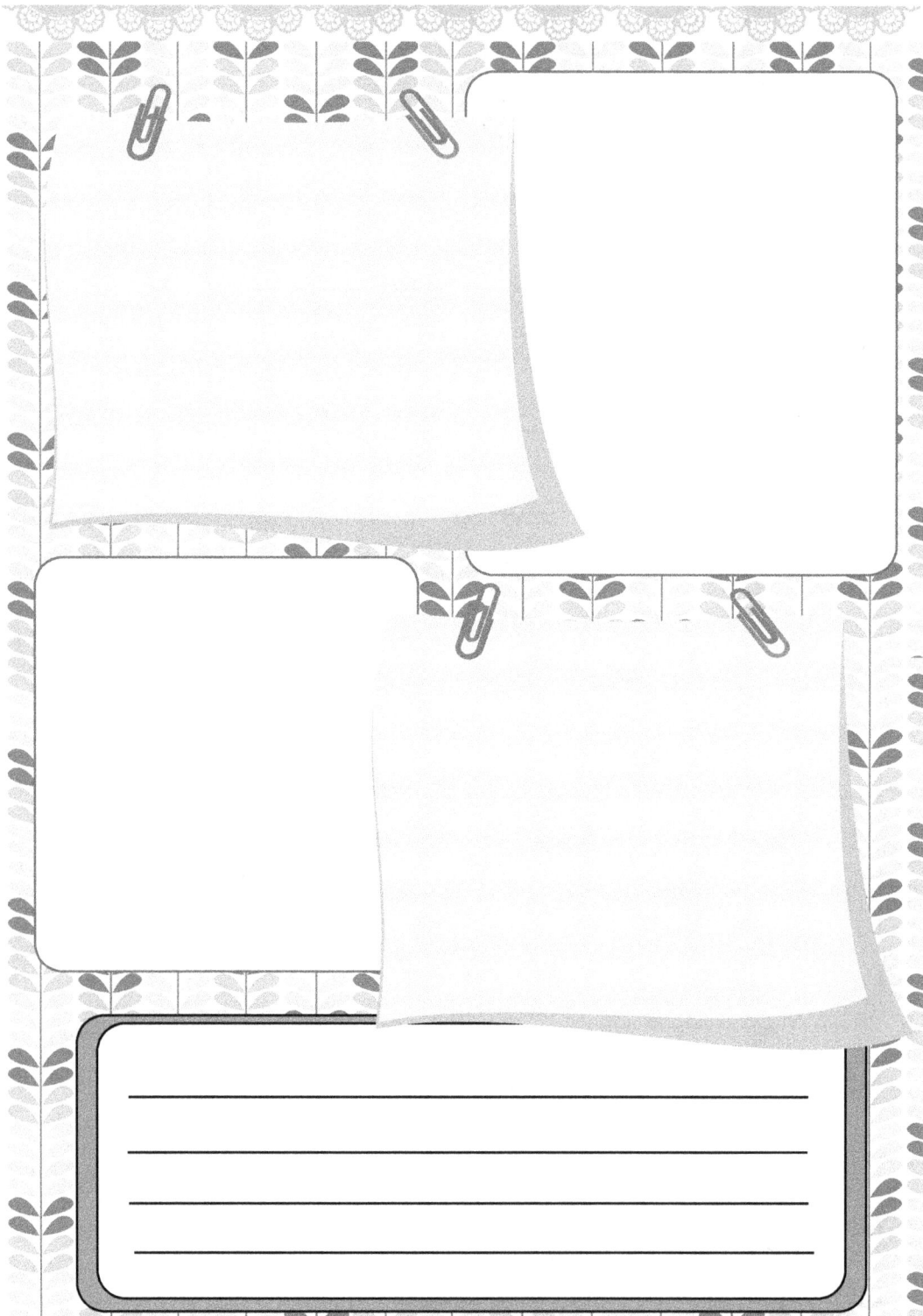

Weekly Planner

Weekly Planner

MONDAY	TUESDAY	WEDNESDAY	To Do List

THURSDAY	FRIDAY	SATURDAY	To Buy List

SUNDAY	To Do List

Weekly Planner

Weekly Planner

Weekly Planner

MONDAY	TUESDAY	WEDNESDAY	To Do List

THURSDAY	FRIDAY	SATURDAY	To Buy List

SUNDAY	To Do List

Weekly Planner

Weekly Planner

Weekly Planner

MONDAY	TUESDAY	WEDNESDAY	To Do List

THURSDAY	FRIDAY	SATURDAY	To Buy List

SUNDAY	To Do List

Weekly Planner

Weekly Planner

Weekly Planner

MONDAY	TUESDAY	WEDNESDAY	To Do List

THURSDAY	FRIDAY	SATURDAY	To Buy List

SUNDAY	To Do List

Weekly Planner

Weekly Planner

Weekly Planner

MONDAY	TUESDAY	WEDNESDAY	To Do List

THURSDAY	FRIDAY	SATURDAY	To Buy List

SUNDAY	To Do List

Weekly Planner

Weekly Planner

Weekly Planner

MONDAY	TUESDAY	WEDNESDAY	To Do List

THURSDAY	FRIDAY	SATURDAY	To Buy List

SUNDAY	To Do List

Weekly Planner

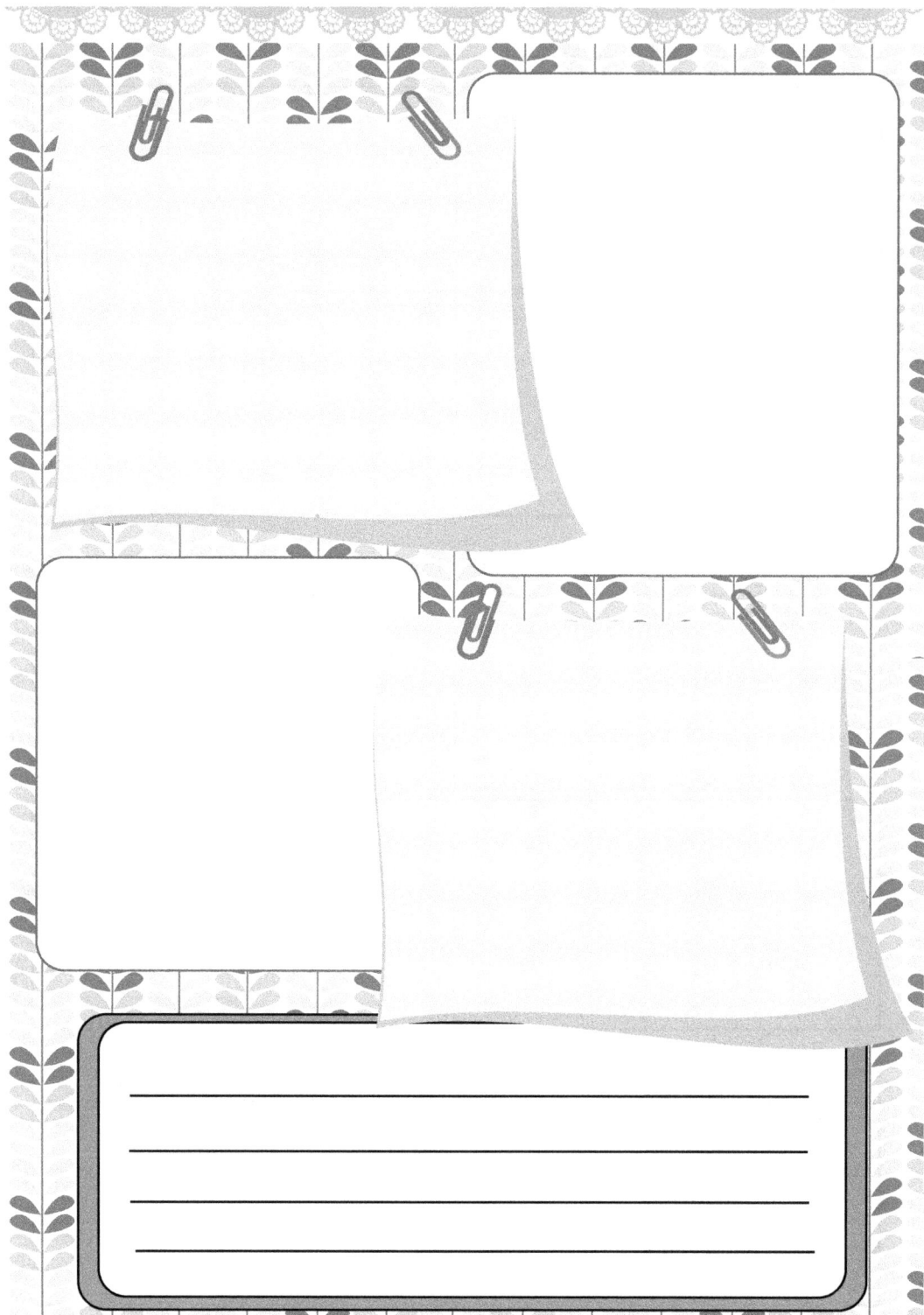

Weekly Planner

Weekly Planner

MONDAY	TUESDAY	WEDNESDAY	To Do List

THURSDAY	FRIDAY	SATURDAY	To Buy List

SUNDAY	To Do List

Weekly Planner

Weekly Planner

Weekly Planner

MONDAY	TUESDAY	WEDNESDAY	To Do List

THURSDAY	FRIDAY	SATURDAY	To Buy List

SUNDAY	To Do List

Weekly Planner

Weekly Planner

Weekly Planner

MONDAY	TUESDAY	WEDNESDAY	To Do List

THURSDAY	FRIDAY	SATURDAY	To Buy List

SUNDAY	To Do List

Weekly Planner

Weekly Planner

Weekly Planner

MONDAY	TUESDAY	WEDNESDAY	To Do List

THURSDAY	FRIDAY	SATURDAY	To Buy List

SUNDAY	To Do List

Weekly Planner

Weekly Planner

Weekly Planner

MONDAY	TUESDAY	WEDNESDAY	To Do List

THURSDAY	FRIDAY	SATURDAY	To Buy List

SUNDAY	To Do List

Weekly Planner

Weekly Planner

Weekly Planner

MONDAY	TUESDAY	WEDNESDAY	To Do List

THURSDAY	FRIDAY	SATURDAY	To Buy List

SUNDAY	To Do List

Weekly Planner

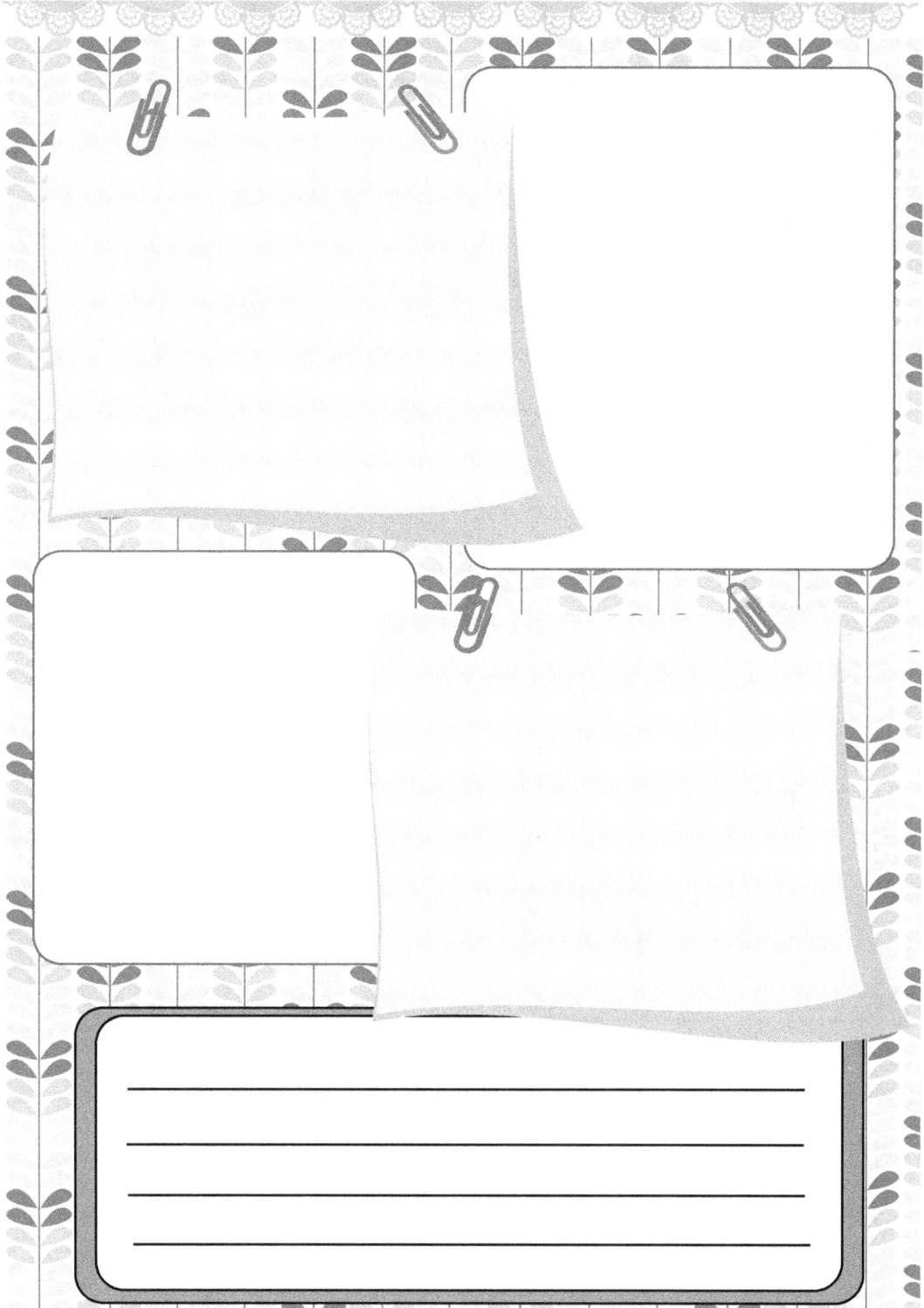

Weekly Planner

Weekly Planner

MONDAY	TUESDAY	WEDNESDAY	To Do List

THURSDAY	FRIDAY	SATURDAY	To Buy List

SUNDAY	To Do List

Weekly Planner

Weekly Planner

Weekly Planner

MONDAY	TUESDAY	WEDNESDAY	To Do List

THURSDAY	FRIDAY	SATURDAY	To Buy List

SUNDAY	To Do List

Weekly Planner

Weekly Planner

Weekly Planner

MONDAY	TUESDAY	WEDNESDAY	To Do List

THURSDAY	FRIDAY	SATURDAY	To Buy List

SUNDAY	To Do List

Weekly Planner

Weekly Planner

Notes